CONFESSIONS:

A Mom's Journey from Hovering to Hope

Eve M. Harrell

Confessions:
A Mom's Journey from Hovering to Hope

Copyright ©2023 by Eve M. Harrell
2nd Edition of the original 2015 publication:
Confessions of a Helicopter Mom

This book or parts thereof may not be reproduced in any form without prior written permission of the author, except as provided by United States of America copyright law.

Unless otherwise noted, All Scripture quotations marked (NIV) are taken from the Holy Bible, New International Version®, NIV®. Copyright © 1973, 1978, 1984, 2011 by Biblica, Inc.™ Used by permission of Zondervan. All rights reserved worldwide. www.zondervan.com The "NIV" and "New International Version" are trademarks registered in the United States Patent and Trademark Office by Biblica, Inc.™

Cover design and photo by Eve M. Harrell

A Daughter's Journey LLC
http://adaughtersjourney.net.

All rights reserved.

DEDICATION

I dedicate this book to my beautiful grandmomma, Sybil LeVan, who exemplified love and grace. I am humbled and honored to have witnessed her life as a life well lived.

To Tony, my loving husband, thank you for sharing your life with me. With you, I have learned to enjoy life and love, more than I could ever ask for in a lifetime. Thank you for encouraging me as I navigate this journey.

To Lee and Lance, thank you for being amazing sons. I am so thankful for the gift I have been given as your mom. You have blessed me in more ways than I can ever express and have taught me the true meaning of unconditional love.

There are many whom I would like to thank for mentoring, teaching, and loving me through this process: John and Linda Owen, Diane LeVan-Lentz, Jennifer Bowser, Patricia Johnson, Amanda Tousel, Julie Swain, Sandy Knap, Tracy Turner, Melanie Craver, Lisa Shumate, Kathini Mutisya, Holly Pastor, and Derik and Meagan Idol.

Lisa Spruell, thank you for loving and accepting me just as I am, you have inspired me to embrace all God has created within me.

To all my girls (you know who you are), thank you for allowing me to work with and serve you. God may not have given me daughters, but I consider each of you my own and am so thankful to have you in my life.

Thank you, Tracy Turner, and Danielle Kitts, who graciously helped me in the crafting of this gift. You have touched my life, and I am so very thankful for your input.

To moms and dads everywhere who suffer from anxiety and worry over the parenting of your children, thank you for the love and sacrifice you give every day to your children and for allowing me to share my experience with you. My prayer is that you, too, will find peace through the message in this book.

Many thanks go to Pastors Kevin Myers, Kevin Queen, and Dan Reiland; thank you for pouring into 12Stone® Church and for teaching us to live life according to God's plan.

To my Heavenly Father, thank you for being my Father, mentor, and flight instructor. Thank you for entrusting me with this beautiful gift of parenthood. Thank you for inspiration. Thank you for grace and for peace. Help me to always point others to you. To you God, we give all glory and praise, the author of our story.

TABLE OF CONTENTS

Dedication	ii
Introduction	v
Chapter 1 – The Realization	1
Chapter 2 – The Challenge	13
Chapter 3 – Parenting 101 The Handbook	33
Chapter 4 – Learning to Love	41
Chapter 5 – Learning to Give	57
Chapter 6 – Get Wisdom	69
Chapter 7 – Learning to Let Go	85
Chapter 8 – Learning to Enjoy the Adventure	103
Chapter 9 – Freedom!	110
Chapter 10 – Redemption	119
Final Thoughts	128
About the Author	130

INTRODUCTION

What is your greatest fear? As a parent, I would find myself bound to the fear of imperfection with hovering as my survival response. What I didn't realize was that fear created whirlwinds and downdrafts, producing anxiety and stress while threatening to take me down and out.

Do you find yourself anxiously hovering over the daily lives of those you love? Or are you firmly planted in their presence? If you answered yes to finding yourself in the anxious state of hovering, you are not alone.

In my own journey, I learned there is another way. Fear does not have to control me. Worry does not have to be a common staple in my vocabulary, and peace is attainable. Grab a journal and join me on a journey full of surprises and detours. Travel with me in the passenger seat as I share practical ways that help me to navigate the lift of life.

My prayer is that you, too, will find the Power that helps us glide through the challenges we face with love and grace while finding peace in the balance.

CONFESSION #1
I TEND TO HOVER.

> Chapter 1
> The Realization

I have always been in awe of helicopters. Close your eyes with me for a moment and experience the whirlwind of air. Feel the propellers whip around as they increase in speed. Listen as the engine powers up the rotors for the ultimate in flight. This machine never fails to create a scene capable of stopping anyone in their tracks. I find it interesting that this feat in flight is used to define the parenting behavior of hovering. Even more revealing was the fact that this behavior is one with which I was quite familiar. Was it the whirlwind created in the wake of the lift-off? Or perhaps the messiness from the debris left behind? Do

I, too, create a scene that would stop someone in their tracks?

OUCH!

It was a cold November night in 2011 when I would unknowingly face a whirlwind. I was forced to shut off the engine of my control and reach up through the blades to the only One who had this hoverer in his hand.

Fast forward to May of 2012, I was sitting in a college orientation once again finding myself within the wake of my own whirlwind. As the College representative advised a roomful of parents that their children were on their own; the fallout created from my own debris began to take shape. "But will my son stay fed through the whole year?" I silently asked myself. The person leading the meeting seemed to hear my anxious thoughts and attempted to lighten the mood by making a reference to helicopter parenting. The nervous laughter around the room seemed to confirm that I wasn't the only one struggling with this conversation.

Confessions: A Mom's Journey from Hovering to Hope

Helicopter parents[1] are so named because, like helicopters, they hover closely overhead, rarely out of reach, whether their children need them or not. When I first heard this term, along with its defining characteristics, I asked my husband if he thought I was such a parent. He looked at me and laughed. I guess I have my answer.

Why are we even having this conversation? Well firstly, I am in no way judging or labeling you as a helicopter parent. I recognize that every parent has a different approach to child-rearing and of course, every child has different needs. But as I sat in this orientation, I realized that if I was struggling with hovering, then perhaps there is more to the conversation for all of us. And so, I did what my Type A personality always does, I began a deep dive study into parenting. What I found was fascinating, and quite revealing if I'm honest. This journey led me down a road to revelation and heartbreak, but more importantly, restoration. And here I am. I would love to share my journey with you. Even

---

[1] http://wikipedia.org/wiki/helicopter_parent

if you don't struggle as I do. There are keys to parenting that I think are helpful to us all.

Let's begin with a simple definition. What does hover mean? The act of hovering means to remain in the air in one place without moving in any direction; to stay very close to a person or place, to stay near a specified point or level.[2] Our first visualization of hovering is, of course, a helicopter. It begs the question, *is hovering a bad thing?*

Sitting in this room of anxious parents, I realized that my sons were not going to be with us much longer. Sadly, I realized I would miss them. The conversations, the laughter, the mommy-son dates, and yes, even the excruciatingly long nights spent waiting for them to come home. There was comfort in knowing that I was entrusted with the care of these two lives. Would all this change in this season?

In May 2014, CBS Money Watch referenced that almost four out of ten Americans between eighteen and twenty-four years old say their parents are involved in their search for employment.[3] In 2016, an interesting report shared the most unusual or surprising behaviors of parents as seen by potential employers of job seekers.[4] How many of these parents sit in the teetering comfort of responsibility? Where do we draw the line between our responsibility and our children's? What challenges enable us to take the reins in areas that perhaps are not ours to take?

Okay, the English lesson is over. If I may, I would like to share a word of encouragement here. This book is not a means to condemn any parent but is my attempt to share thoughts from my own personal experiences. There is something cathartic about having someone hold your hand and say, I see you, I've been where you are. Take my hand and let's walk this journey together. Consider me that person. Regardless of what society

---

[2] www.merriam-webster.com/dictionary/hover
[3] www.cbsnews.com/news/how-helicopter-parents-are-muscling-in-on-kids-job-searches/
[4] https://press.roberthalf.com/2016-08-16-Mom-To-Employer-Do-You-Mind-If-I-Sit-In-On-My-Sons-Interview

says, we are in this together and we are never alone. Now let's start walking.

How Did I Get Here?

I have wanted to be a mom for as long as I can remember, practicing as young as the age of eleven as I cared for my sisters. Then, at the tender age of nineteen, I was given the most incredible gift of my life. I can remember during an easy pregnancy, thinking that I would never know all there was to being a good parent. Anxiety set in—would I be a good mom? What if I dropped him? What if he became ill, and I couldn't make him well? What if he doesn't like me?

> Fear would overcome me. The need for control would be born through my insecurities. Worry would guide my decisions. Stress would become a familiar friend. My thoughts would become obsessed with the negative. Can you relate? This was the beginning of my helicopter days.

This causes me to ponder, how have previous generations parented their children?

Let's Take a Look.

Over the last 500 years, we have watched the role of a parent in their child's life change considerably. In medieval Europe, many children were under their parent's wing only until the age of seven or fourteen at the most. It would be at this age that they would be sent out to work as a servant or for educational training for the remainder of their adolescent years. This was considered not only to fill a financial need for the family but also an opportunity for the child to gain experience from someone outside of the parental unit.[5]

In the 1800s, children were seen as small adults expected to grow up quickly. Labor and household work were primary activities in a child's life, chores designed to provide for the family while building character and grit. Children would be mentored by

---

[5] http://www.sarahwoodbury.com/child-rearing-in-the-middle-ages/

older adults who would share their life and work experience. Educational instruction, including reading, writing, and math, were typically basic and secondary considerations.[6]

Toward the end of the 1800s, we begin to see a societal shift in the view of the role of a child in the home and workplace. We see two important groups develop to provide for the advocacy of the welfare of a child. The American Pediatric Society was established with "the objective to bring together men and women for the advancement of the study of children and their diseases, for the prevention of illness and the promotion of health in childhood, for the promotion of pediatric education and research, and to honor those who, by their contributions to pediatrics, have aided in its advancement."[7] The National Parent Teacher Association (PTA) was founded to empower families and communities to advocate for all children.[8]

---

[6] http://www.ehow.com/info_8084427_childrearing-practices-1800s.html

[7] http://wikipedia.org/wiki/American_Pediatric_Society

[8] www.pta.org/about/content.cfm?ItemNumber=944

Confessions: A Mom's Journey from Hovering to Hope

The next century would reflect a great change in the trajectory of the child-parent relationship. Benjamin Spock would open our eyes to the world of the child and intuitive parenting in 1946 with his book The Common Sense Book of Baby and Child Care, encouraging moms to trust their instincts related to parenting.[9] The 1900s in general would present a myriad of scientific and psychological opinions regarding the role of a parent and the rights of a child. Consequently, this would result in the definition of several parenting styles including "attachment parenting." Was this the beginning of an age that created a chasm in the life of a child—a chasm that needed to be filled?

In the present day, we live in a century of increasing technological advances. Forty years ago, our parents were happy to send us out after breakfast to be in before dark, but now we find children replacing fun with fads, books with social media, and physical activity

---

[9] http://www.positive-parenting-ally.com/benjamin-spock.html

with tablets and video games. What have we filled this chasm with?

As I ponder these revelations, a few questions come to my hovering mind:

- Is my fear of letting go creating a need to compensate for loss?
- Is there something else gaining influence over my children that frightens me?
- Can I redirect my thoughts from the negative to the positive?
- What about love? Is there a difference between loving my child and hovering over them?

One more thought before we dive into the challenges of parenting. It is recorded that the Spirit of God hovered over the waters in the beginning (Genesis 1:2). What does God say about hovering?
What if we had a manual to answer all our questions?

Personal Confession

Have you ever found yourself hovering over your children's lives?

Ask God to reveal this to you and ask him to show you what in your own life creates the need to hover.

Feel free to journal your thoughts here._____

_____

_____

_____

_____

_____

_____

_____

_____

_____

Confessions: A Mom's Journey from Hovering to Hope

CONFESSION #2—I DO NOT ALWAYS KNOW WHAT I AM DOING.

> Chapter 2
> The Challenge

As we navigated the prayer trail on that dark November night, I was in awe of the soft white lights that led us down the path. One thing that I knew without a doubt was that I needed to be guided on this path, or else I would lose my way. Why? Because I didn't know where I was going.

Do you have days when you just don't know where to go or what to do? Is it a struggle to find the right path or make the right decision? Does stability seem like an impossible feat?

Yeah, me too.

The Challenge of Positive Thinking

I previously shared my tendency toward negative thinking. For example, I feared that I would not be a good parent and worried whether my son would accept or reject me. Where do these thoughts originate? Why are my thoughts so critical?

I am a snoozer; is anyone with me? I set my alarm at 5:45 every morning and over the next forty-five minutes, my alarm will go off at least five times. Yep, it goes off every nine minutes, like clockwork. At 6:30, when I finally decide to jump out of bed, my very next action will set the trajectory for the rest of my day.

> Pause here for a moment—what is your first action? What is your first thought for the day? Honestly, for many years I would spend forty-five minutes mentally running through all the things I had to do that day. And very much like a rock

that picks up speed down a slippery slope, all these thoughts would compound until at 6:30, stress was already infringing on a new day in front of me. Do you, too, suffer from the onslaught of the "thought avalanche" as I do?

Chip Ingram shares a commentary on the book of Galatians as written by John Stott in Good to Great in God's Eyes: "Sow a thought, reap an action. Sow an action, reap a habit. Sow a habit, reap a character. Sow a character, reap a destiny. Eventually, we will be the product of our thinking."[10] Whoa, this gives me pause. My thoughts are powerful. The control of my thoughts becomes the joystick that can transport me up into a positive mind-set or down into a negative mind-set. So how can we practically apply this to life?

"Above all else, guard your heart, for everything you do flows from it" (Proverbs 4:23). This is advice from the

---

[10] *Good to Great in God's Eyes*—Chip Ingram –2007

same God who hovered over the waters at creation. This advice is meant to protect our heart and thoughts.

Okay God, so what should I do when the thought avalanche begins? In his gentle whisper, I heard, "Daughter I breathed my life into you. At this moment, greet me, breathe me in, thank me for the day, for life, for love. You can ask me for anything that aligns with my will. How about asking me to guard your heart and your thoughts which have the power to give or steal your joy? Yes, Daughter, this may mean that you need to hit the snooze button one less time. Allow me to use these extra nine minutes to set your day on the right course."

Wow, what a revelation! I could intentionally control my thoughts! God was going to help me set my day! But it begins with a choice.

To take this a step further, I had to consider spontaneous thoughts throughout the day. Admittedly, unexpected interruptions can create quite a blind spot that can take my spontaneous thoughts down a path of no return.

"Mom, I'm not coming home." Phone calls such as this filled me with angst. The journey we were walking was filled with moments of disappointment. I'm not coming home would result in a thought that sounded like, I'm never coming home. Disappointment would lead to anxiety and stress from a single negative thought that threatened to steal my joy.

"What do I do, God?"

Who has time in moments such as this to dissect their thoughts? Ah, time to reveal the secret of choice. I have a choice to dig into this negative thought, focus on it, and allow emotion to lead me like a helicopter spinning out of control; or I can take a deep breath, pray for wisdom, and speak truth over the thought. It's time to guard my heart again. What is the truth? I am a child of God, fearfully and wonderfully made in his image, with a purpose and a plan to give me hope and a future. He entrusted me with my sons and with the wisdom to lead them. In this example, the action reaped is a moment of grace for me as the Father leads me into peace. Oh, and guess what? God always meets us where we are, but he never leaves us there. He had an extra dose of grace for my son and I as we navigated peace and patience in the wait.

Now, how do I turn this into a habit that reaps peace? I find intentional reminders to be helpful. As an example, I have the quote referenced before, "Above all else, guard your heart, for everything you do flows from it" on my desk at work. Surrounding myself with reminders of truth helps when spontaneous thoughts find their way into my blind spot.

Speaking of intentionality, it is just as important to train our minds to recognize negative thoughts before they creep in. As I am faced with challenges, I recognize patterns in my response. Patterns, when realized, guide me to guard my heart. The example referenced above would create a moment of hopelessness if I wasn't careful. By recognizing this feeling before I react, I can train myself to stop and give myself a moment to speak the truth, while praying for wisdom and strength, before I give in to hopelessness. It is important to understand my tendency in a fight-or-flight moment, so I can be intentional in my response and allow it to become a moment of hope, for me and my son. And through this, God turns a negative into a positive.

All through the day, we have the choice to allow our thoughts to take over and affect our behavior, or we can take control of them. The result of our taking our thoughts captive and allowing God to enter in, creates a positive experience for ourselves and for everyone around us. I must admit this was a game-changer for me. For years, I allowed negative influences to enter my mind and create insecurity, fear, worry, and stress. If I were a betting person, I'd bet that ruminating over these negative influences allowed a seed of hovering to take root.

The Challenge of Making Decisions:

Remember when you were a child? Life was full of cartoons, afternoon naps, and playtime. My parents' job seemed so easy: feed me and love me. That sounds easy, right? How many of us raised our hands when we were young and said, "Me, me; I want to be a parent!" It seems to be ingrained in us to want to be a mom or a dad. At a young age, we learn to feed a baby doll from a bottle or rock them to sleep. Or perhaps, we learn to protect the fort. As parents, we find that decisions come in all shapes and sizes.

- Which bottle is best for digestion?
- Which Pre-K will most shape our young one's mind?
- Should I send my children to public school or private?
- Whom should we allow our children to hang out with?
- What college will allow my child to prosper and succeed?

There are so many decisions to be made as a parent. How do we decide? Whom do we turn to? Is there a right or wrong decision? Candidly, I will share that this book is not one that will give you these answers.

However, in the chapters to follow, I would like to point you in a direction where you can make these decisions on your own, in confidence.

The Challenge of Communication

Communication is challenging for all of us. Through my meager experience in parenting, I am learning that the casualties created when communication is lacking can be fatal. We always have the best of intentions, right? However, the consequence for a lack of communication can be a lack of trust and respect between all family members.

> I will honestly admit that I haven't always respected my husband or his decisions. Quite often, in fact, I would make both small and large decisions, which we should both have agreed upon. Whether due to fear, uncertainty, or time constraints, this error in judgment created stress in both my life and in my relationship with my

husband. Do you struggle with this as well? There is hope, my friend; grace cuts a path through the weeds of our fear, stress, and insecurity to a clearing of peace.

One day I asked God, "What does communication look like?" His answer, "Daughter, I created relationships, and in each relationship is the beauty of "unity." The Unity of I Am created the heavens and the earth. The Unity of God and man named every animal in the garden. The unity of man and woman through the anointing of my hand delivered future generations. Unity through communication births thoughts which are true, noble, right, pure, lovely, and admirable (Philippians 4:8). When communication is respected, unity is found, and life gets done."

Wow, what a revelation! From the very beginning, God unified us and prepared us for communication giving us the tools we need to communicate effectively. With this revelation, I recognize the importance to discuss every decision made in the family.

What does this look like in the realm of parenting?

First, decide up front which decisions can be made "on the fly" and which decisions require agreement from both parents. For decisions that are made "on the fly," discuss the best way to handle them ahead of time. For example, Eddie may come to Mom and ask if he can go to his friend's house after school. Mom is probably not going to contact Dad and ask his permission; however, Mom and Dad can set specific rules about homework, when Eddie is to be home for dinner, and so forth. An example of a decision requiring mutual agreement is when Cindy asks Dad for $200 for a school project. Dad and Mom have discussed previously that anything over $100 must be communicated and agreed upon. So in this case, Dad would contact Mom and seek a consensual agreement on the funds. Then communicate these decisions with your children. Don't be afraid to tell them to be patient and wait for an answer. Encourage them to understand that their question is worthy of your best answer, which means they must learn:

- To wait patiently for an answer.
- That your answer is your "Final answer."
- To respect that no is not a dirty word.
- What is negotiable and what is non-negotiable.
- That parental competition in decision-making is not an option.

As parents, when we respect one another and share in decision-making, we can teach our children one of the most important lessons in their lifetime: how to communicate. You will find that there is great freedom in communication. When boundaries are set, parenting becomes a team effort and no longer a super-human effort to accomplish everything on your own. For those who must make all decisions on your own, know that I have great love and respect for you. Parenting is hard and fulfilling the responsibility of both parents is nothing short of amazing. For you, while communication with a partner may not be possible, just as important I think, is to communicate boundaries ahead of time with your children. Then stick to them.

For all of us, remember that in making any decision, whether individually or in community, God, our Heavenly Father, is ready to help. Learning to communicate our requests to him through prayer allows him to guide us in our decisions and teaches our children that he can be trusted. And even if you miss the mark and your plans do not meet God's purpose initially, remember that his purpose will prevail (Proverbs 19:21). He can work through our wrong decisions and grow us in the process.

The Challenge of Choice

In the beginning, God shares the story of Adam and Eve. In God's perfect creation, he sought a relationship. He created two individuals to whom he gave the gift of free will. He gave them a choice to obey or disobey. We all know how this story ended, with man and woman choosing their own way instead of taking the path that God laid out for them (Genesis 3). It is my belief that God experienced a bit of sadness over Adam and Eve's regretful choice to choose their will over his direction. Then he watched as his chosen people continuously choose their own vices over the blessings he had for them, but he had to let them make their own choices. Why? Maybe first, we should ponder another question, how often do we choose our will over God's?

As I see it, there are typically seven steps in life that every generation experiences:

- Birth.
- Independence, when we realize the freedom at our fingertips.
- Rebellion, when we realize that our will can be greater than those who are trying to teach us.
- Discipline, when we walk outside of our moral boundaries and face consequences.
- Regret, when we realize that our will may not be the best course of action.
- Acceptance of obedience, once we mature and realize that we are part of a bigger picture.

- Death.

Along the way, we all have ups and downs, bumps and bruises, regression, and progression. Some of us may be smart enough to skip a couple of these steps. But typically, that map is the same for all of us. I wonder; does this mean that our children follow in our influential footsteps—good, bad, or ugly?

In the seventh grade, I signed up for the science fair. My project was to present the physical effects of drugs on the body. I researched all kinds of drugs, including illegal drugs, alcohol, and cigarette smoking. I became quite the expert. I didn't do so well in the "science" fair (it apparently wasn't considered science). However, this project was a life-changing experience for me personally that influenced my future life choices. Not only did this affect the choices that I made in my life, but I also made a conscious decision to pour what I learned into my own children. I thought for sure that they would make the same choice that I did. I was wrong.

When we decide to have children, we first think that we can shield our children from making bad choices. We decide, "Well I'm not going to allow Betty to hang out with that crowd" or "I'm going to teach Johnny to play football." So, what do you do when Betty becomes friends with that crowd in school, or Johnny doesn't like football? You cannot be with them every moment of every day, nor can you decide their likes and dislikes. While you can set boundaries for them and give them instruction to stay within those boundaries; ultimately, they make their own choices.

Teaching our children that there are consequences for choice becomes critical. Our taking personal responsibility for their choices will not help them in the long run.

Over the course of my parenting, I have made a lot of mistakes. I've learned; however, that the mistakes I face point me to the One who promises to help me through the challenge. One, who promised that when we "trust in the Lord with all your heart and lean not on your own understanding; in all your ways submit to him, he will make your paths straight (Proverbs 3:5–6)." Our Heavenly Father serves literally as a "Stabilizer Bar," meeting us where we are and helping us smooth out the challenges in life. You, too, can trust him.

Know this my friend; there is hope in the challenge. God allows challenges in our life, challenges that help us to grow but may seem insurmountable at the time. Yet later, we find that these challenges serve to guide us into our greatest achievements. We find peace when we come to the realization that a challenge is nothing more than a hill to climb, guiding us to the other side. This realization becomes beneficial to us in that we recognize we are not alone. God grants grace with an impartation of wisdom when we make an error in judgment. He entrusted us with these bundles of joy and is fully ready and able to help us step into our calling. But we need to give him our hand.

You may be asking yourself, "Okay, when does this realization happen?" I cannot answer for you, and for myself, I'm still processing. But keep reading and maybe we'll find it together.

Back to that manual, what does God expect of us when he trusts us with these beautiful bundles of joy? He didn't give us a handbook, or did he?

Personal Confession

Do you allow God to help you with parenting? Do you trust that he will provide wisdom when you need it?

Do you struggle with maintaining positive thoughts?

Where do you need to guard your heart and reject negative thoughts? A tip that has helped me is to find a handful of bible verses relevant to something you need God to pour into you, write them on a sticky note, and place them in locations where they are readily available for you to read daily. Allow God to "write his Word on your heart" as you read them every day.

What decisions and/or choices in your own life do you need to give to him, trusting that he will guide and direct you and your child?

Do you struggle with communicating with your partner and/or your children?

Pray for God's wisdom to help you through these challenges. You will find beautiful grace and mercy on your knees.

Feel free to journal your thoughts here._____

CONFESSION #3—I OFTEN FIND MYSELF SEEKING CONTROL RATHER THAN WISE INSTRUCTION.

Chapter 3
Parenting 101
The Handbook

I thought I could fix it. There, I said it. Prior to that fateful night in November, I tried everything I could to change the trajectory in which my family was headed. And I wasn't the only one. As we walked down the trail, I could see others kneeling before the throne of God who appeared to be in a similar place. We had all expended every tool in our toolbox to attempt to fix that which was broken.

Do you remember when you studied Parenting 101? Do you remember your teacher? Do you remember the grade you received? Did you pass or fail? As far as I know, my high school did not offer Parenting 101. How many times have we heard, "They should teach that in school," or "You must have a license to drive a car, but not to parent a child"?

Parenting becomes the class itself that we provide to our children. You may be asking, but how do we prepare? We spend valuable years being mentored by our own parents, aka "teachers," who strive to provide the best they can for us, love us, give us the things we need, and teach us how to be morally responsible people. The job of a parent is to raise adults and prepare them for life.

Now that's a concept. Do you mean to tell me that I am learning on the job? Training the trainer? If you are like me, you may find yourself trying to take control, only because you feel afraid that you don't know it all and certainly don't have all the answers. This begs the question, is taking control a dirty word, even if our intentions are good? Do we get lost in translation believing that being "in control" is the same as being "in charge?"

What is the difference? To be in control of something means that you are directing its every move and are responsible for the result. To be in charge of something or someone means that you are only responsible for teaching, guiding, and helping them to ultimately take over. If our job is to raise adults who will ultimately be responsible for their own lives, then we recognize that we are not in control at all. Instead, we are placed in charge of preparing our children for adulthood and the challenges they, too, will face. A wise friend once said, "I can't take all the credit for my children, and I can't take all the blame, either." This means that we can accept the responsibility we are given to take charge and strive to become the good parents that God called us to be while allowing our children to take responsibility for themselves.

A question- What do you think makes up good parents?

Here are some of my thoughts:

- A good parent loves.
- A good parent is giving.
- A good parent is willing to set an example and be a mentor.
- A good parent helps their child to see their value.
- A good parent is willing to make sacrifices for their child to succeed.
- A good parent is willing to allow their child to experience consequences.
- A good parent is someone who recognizes that by bringing someone into this world, they are leaving a mark of themselves to carry on long after they are gone.
- A good parent is willing to let go so their child can become who they were created to be.

Wow, just listing these, I'm feeling a bit discouraged. Will I ever be a "good parent?" If you feel as I do, may I encourage you not to put the book down just yet?

What we all can realize, and even rest in, is that parenting is hard. Parenting can bless us with our greatest joy, and it can also bring our greatest sorrow. **A humbling experience, parenting <u>gives</u> us a small example of God's love for us.** He is the One who continually sets the ultimate example of being the perfect parent. Wait, so God is our example, you ask? Well, yes, God is the perfect example of parenthood at its finest! He created Adam and Eve, knowing they would defy Him. He brought a people together whom he knew would walk away from him (Jeremiah 31:32). The Psalmist says that he knit us in our mother's womb (Psalm 139:13); he knew us before anyone ever did. He sent his Son to die for all of us who, even today, continue to turn our back on him so that we can follow our own will and live the way we think life should be lived. But he loved us anyway. **He loves us anyway.** Wow, what a sacrifice. I could never live up to this perfect example of unconditional love, could I?

Going back to the seven steps of life, maybe, just maybe, these steps are placed in front of us so we can catch a glimpse of unconditional love and, in time, learn when to open the throttle to full capacity or depress the pedal when it comes to parenting. To truly learn to love a person, there must be sacrifice, humility, and a willingness to serve. Yes, there will be mistakes. But the beauty of our life, a "work in progress," is that we get to watch the Master at work. He is the perfect example because God is love. "And so, we know and rely on the love God has for us. God is love. Whoever lives in love lives in God, and God in them" (1 John 4:16).

How can we learn to be good parents and learn not to hover?" Well, I think it all starts with love, trust, and learning to relinquish control. Oh, and the Parenting Handbook? Our Father left us the perfect Handbook in His Word, the Holy Bible, our Father's love story written to give us life as he promised in John 10:10b, "I have come that they may have life, and have it to the full."

Personal Confession

Do you struggle with the need to be the "Good and Perfect Parent?"

Recognize that God not only blessed you with these beautiful bundles of joy, but he trusted you with them as well, promising to guide and direct you in your journey as a parent.

Pray that he will help you relinquish control to him and will instruct you in how to be the parent he called you to be, providing you with the strength and wisdom to fill this purpose.

Feel free to journal your thoughts here.

_____

_____

_____

_____

_____

Confessions: A Mom's Journey from Hovering to Hope

CONFESSION #4—I FIND IT DIFFICULT TO LOVE UNCONDITIONALLY.

> Chapter 4
> Learning to Love

If I couldn't fix the broken pieces, did this mean that I didn't love enough? That was the question I found myself asking over and over when the whirlwind seemed to take over my circumstance.

While growing up, my heart longed for all the things my friends had. I grew up in a home rich in love and hugs, but we struggled financially. My dad worked two, sometimes three, jobs to make ends meet. My mom taught me how to hug, and my dad taught me how to be faithful to where I place my heart. The two of them shared the values and the love that I am thankful to have today. As the oldest of five sisters, I learned at a very early age how to take care of others. Looking back on that time of my life, I can remember feeling like I was missing out on something—on everything. Now I recognize this was shaping me to be the person I am today.

Can we love unconditionally? Honestly, I can say that there have been times in my life when loving unconditionally has been difficult. Finding the humility to let go of control and love the way God teaches is hard work. Hovering seems much easier than learning to encourage my children to ascend in their own forward flight. Why is that? Is hovering comfortable, I wonder? Or am I just plain inexperienced in love?

I'll share a lighter example of what I mean: Homework was a stressful topic in our house. One child had to be chased to do it (or turn it in). The other was disciplined and never needed reminding. For my son, who struggled with this discipline, I felt it my responsibility to remind him repeatedly. I would stay in constant contact with teachers even to obtain testing and project dates. Looking back now, was this love or hovering? Who was in control of turning in his homework?

What is love? Wikipedia defines love as "a virtue representing all of human kindness, compassion, and affection."[11] Love is a noun and, most importantly, a verb in pure form as designed and modeled by our Heavenly Father who is Love. Love seems to be an easy word to throw around these days. But how do we love? Where does love originate? Is there a right or wrong way to love our children?

In the first chapter of Genesis in the Bible, we watch as our Creator spent six days creating the heavens and the earth. He formed light, water, land, stars, animals, and finally mankind. Verse 27 tells us that he created man and woman "in his own image." Great care was made to create a self-sustaining planet that would provide for his beloved creation. In verse 31, God calls all that he had made "very good." Chapter two goes on to share how God "breathed into man's nostrils the breath of life" creating a living being. **We have a Creator, a**

Father who is hands-on and loves us unconditionally!

Now, let's look at what Jesus, God's son, said about love. Jesus tells us to, "Love the Lord your God with all your heart and with all your soul and with all your mind and with all your strength" (Mark 12:30). So, for us to truly understand love, we must understand how God first loved us, his creation. "This is Love, not that we loved God, but that he loved us and sent his Son as an atoning sacrifice for our sins" (1 John 4:10).

God loved us first.

Mark goes on to share Jesus' words, "The second is this, love your neighbor as yourself. There is no commandment greater than these" (Mark 12:31). Paul goes on to explain:

> Love is patient, love is kind, it does not envy, it does not boast, it is not proud. It does not dishonor others, it is not

---

[11] http://wikipedia.org/wiki/love

> self-seeking, it is not easily angered, and
> it keeps no record of wrongs. Love does
> not delight in evil but rejoices with the
> truth. It always protects, always trusts,
> always hopes, and always perseveres.
> Love never fails (1 Corinthians 13:4–8).

If I can be transparent, I hang my head as I read these. I know that Jesus willingly and courageously gave his life so I could live. He set the greatest example of love here on earth. He taught us how to live and how to love. But when I read this standard of love, I feel very under-qualified. But what if changing our perspective is the point? To take a quote from my pastor, "You don't really know God until he is loving people through you."[12]

Before he was arrested, Jesus prays a beautiful corporate prayer in the Garden of Gethsamene. One that reflects the very heart of God:

---

[12] Kevin Myers, Senior Pastor 12Stone® Church

> My prayer is not for them alone. I pray
> also for those who will believe in me
> through their message, that all of them
> may be one, Father, just as you are in
> me and I am in you. May they also be in
> us so that the world may believe that
> you have sent me (John 17:20–21).

During a class in Christian Theology, our professor explained that God the Father, the Son, and the Holy Spirit are all One, described as the Trinity, aka the Triune God. Honestly, this is a difficult concept to wrap my brain around: three persons in one God. There is something of this special relationship that I didn't recognize until it was pointed out to me. If God is love, then this love is encompassed within the Father, the Son, and the Holy Spirit, right? In this prayer shared with us by the Apostle John, Jesus prays to God asking that we believe so that we also may be one, as the Father is in the Son and the Son in the Father, so that we become one in them.

Light Bulb!

So, when we receive the love of God firsthand, we are then able to share it with those he places in our path. God loves **through** us. Talk about the circle of life—one big circle of love! Let's break this down into our generation today. Consider your response in each situation:

1. Love is patient—Five-year-old Johnny writes his ABCs on the wall and blames it on two-year-old Kimmy (True story).
2. Love is Kind—Betty falls and bumps her knee, leaving a boo-boo for Mommy to kiss.
3. Love does not envy—Your best friend from high school has two beautifully behaved children who never talk back, cry in a grocery store, or (dare I say) dirty their new white shirt on the first day of school.
4. Love does not boast—Christopher learns to ride a bike. In response, you share with everyone that because of you, he is now mobile.
5. Love is not proud—Cindy Lou makes the volleyball team at school, and again you

must share with your Facebook friends about how if it weren't for you, she never would have joined in the first place.

6. Love does not dishonor others—Bobby gets into a fight at school, and your first thought is to go over and take out the other boy's father.

7. Love is not self-seeking—Your husband comes home from work, and Mary runs to him saying "Daddy, Daddy, I missed you," after you have spent all day cooking, cleaning, and caring for her.

8. Love is not easily angered—Joey comes home after curfew.

9. Love keeps no record of wrongs—In a discussion over grades, accusations fly regarding Johnny's previous lack of attention in his studies.

10. Love does not delight in evil but rejoices with the truth—Mary shares with you that she took a pack of bubble gum from the local convenience store, resulting in the

need to return and an explanation of right and wrong.
11. Love always protects—Mikey decides the pretty orange burner on the stove needs a handprint.
12. Love always trusts—Robby comes to you on Saturday night and asks, "Mom, can I please have the keys to the car?"
13. Love always hopes—Amy calls to give the wonderful news, "Mom, he asked me to marry him!"
14. Love always perseveres—Teddy has to go through chemo for the second time.
15. Love never fails—Chris calls and says, "Mom, I'm in jail."

If you are like me and think these are near to impossible to fulfill, I have hope for you. Learning to love unconditionally means that we must let go to allow God to guide the situation and love through us, especially when we don't know what to do, even if we don't like the consequence. One morning, after reading this passage, I asked, "God, how can I ever live up to this teaching?" In his beautiful and quiet manner, he said, "When you can't, remember that I can." Perhaps, this is the truth of love never fails.

What do you think Jesus would do in these situations? Remember, he was the One who truly taught us the meaning of the love given us by our Heavenly Father. We have stories, including the woman at the well, the raising of Lazarus, Jesus inviting himself to Zacchaeus' house to join him for dinner, Jesus walking on water patiently calling Peter to do the same, and the ultimate sacrifice ever given on the Cross. In all these moments, Jesus is fully present. He is completely in touch with those he loves, values, teaches, and even dies for. Imagine him in a state of forward flight while maintaining a constant altitude as we look into his eyes and recognize the heart of God and his incredible love for us. So, where do we begin?

First, I think it's important to begin at the source. When you look at a body of water, you know that the source of that water had to come from somewhere. We learned that God is love, which means that he is the source of our love. So, we start there. Seek him first every day, and when you feel spent, emptied of love, and exhausted, go to the well of Living Water and allow him to fill you up.

Second, good parenting does not mean perfect parenting. None of us are perfect; only One earned that distinction. We must accept that we will never be perfect in this lifetime. When you fall, allow him to pick you back up and keep going.

Third, make quality time for the little things, such as:

1. Making breakfast for the family.
2. Taking children to the park.
3. Hugs—daily hugs.
4. Conversations, lots of them.
5. Putting the smart-phone or tablet down at dinner and listening to the events of the day as they are shared around the table.
6. Being available when Tommy needs help with his math homework or Sally wants to play with dolls.

7. Reading bedtime stories.
8. Praying over and teaching your children to pray.

To be fully present, willing to listen, and in touch with your children, creates a bond stronger than anything we could ever imagine. Yes, it is true that being a parent can be a daunting challenge. But taking time to create memories will stamp moments forever etched on your heart and on the hearts of your children. Through these moments, you begin to recognize there is a greater Power who lifts these relationships to a beautiful altitude. His unconditional love gives you the strength to persevere and never fail.

In 2014, my pastor Kevin Myers released a book called The Home Run Life. In it, he taught some practical ways to live the life to the full that Jesus has for us. A sermon was born from this book called "Home Run Kids." In this sermon, he shared a couple of thoughts, which spoke volumes to me.

- Parenting takes intentional time, talk and truth.

- Whatever gets little time develops very little.
- We want rewards but with very little investment.
- You're either going to direct or neglect.
- We all have the same time but not all the same values.
- What are your time choices teaching your kids?"[13]

What are our choices teaching our kids? Is our "hovering" keeping us from being able to be fully present in their lives? In my example of hovering over homework, a better choice would have been to set a specific time and location. Then, I should have asked if my son understood the assignment and needed anything while trusting him to complete and turn in his homework without a reminder. And if he didn't, the consequences would be his and not mine.

Our intentionality shows God's love. Through his love, he restores the influence lost in the overbearing nature

---

[13] "Home Run Kids"—Kevin Myers—4/27/2014

of "attachment parenting." Children are very quick to forgive, and trust is easily rebuilt when love is in action.

Now we come to a pinnacle. You may be asking, "How do I love like this?" You may have been raised in a home where unconditional love was never shared. You may think that to show love, you must hover over your children's lives. Well, I can tell you, it's never too late to learn to love as Jesus loved and to set your relationship into a forward flight.

Personal Confession

What in the "Love is/is not" definitions in this chapter do you struggle with?

Do you struggle with your time choices?

Admit this struggle to God and allow him to pour his love into you, teaching you how to love as he loves.

Feel free to journal your thoughts here._____

_____

_____

_____

_____

_____

_____

_____

_____

_____

Confessions: A Mom's Journey from Hovering to Hope

CONFESSION #5
SOMETIMES I GIVE TO COMPENSATE FOR WHAT I CAN'T DO.

> Chapter 5
> Learning to Give

If I can't fix it, maybe I should give more. This was another thought that I had over and over as I faced the whirlwind of my circumstance.

In chapter four, we learned how Jesus taught us to love. Now we will look at the necessity of learning how to give. Jesus shares with us in the Lord's Prayer that when we pray, we are to ask our Father to, "Give us today our daily bread" (Matthew 6:11). Some may see this literally as sustenance, others may see this as our material needs, and still others may see this as God pouring himself into us through his Word. It's fair to say that Jesus is instructing us to ask for all our needs, wouldn't you agree? And in recognizing all our needs, we begin to recognize the eternal gifts we can give, such as faith, value, diligence, and serving others.

The Gift of Faith

In 2013, I had the amazing opportunity to travel with the students in our youth group to Haiti. We went to a little town called Cercady. To be honest, I had no idea of what to expect. I did not go in with any expectations except to serve as the hands and feet of Jesus. Never in my life would I have imagined that they would serve me. God performed a doozy of a miracle in my life that summer.

In Cercady, there was no running water or medical clinic. Children as young as four years old would take a two-hour walk every morning on a rocky mountain road to fill up a bucket of water for the day. This water was used for cooking, cleaning, and drinking. Their nightly dinner was beans and rice. They lived on dirt floors that they kept immaculately clean. Do you want to know what they prayed for every morning? Everything, yes even the beans and rice.

And best of all, they had love. The love described in chapter four, the love described by Jesus, was in this town in droves, and their gift to us, a group of Americans who thought they were coming to serve them, was to love us, too. Their gift to us was to call us family. Their gift to us was to welcome us to their homes as they taught us what Jesus truly meant when he said to "love your neighbor." Their gift to us was to teach us about true faith.

So, what was different about this little town? One, their faith was incredibly strong. Remember how they prayed for everything? Not only did they ask, but they also believed! In Matthew, Jesus taught his disciples that if they "have faith as small as a mustard seed, you can say to this mountain, 'move from here to there,' and it will move. Nothing will be impossible for you" (Matthew 17:20). These beautiful people believed the mountain would move. The gift of faith given to your children will last longer than any monetary gift.

Two, I think they each gave their time to one another in relationship and community. The desire of Cercady to have running water and a medical clinic brought them together to prayerfully create a game plan to bring these to fruition. They recognized a need to work together to bring about improvement while sacrificing their own personal desires for those of the community.

This experience helped me to realize that as a recovering helicopter mom, giving my children everything they ask for can be detrimental to their character growth and could result in an all-too-certain crash and burn scenario. In a little town called Cercady, children were not given everything they wanted, and, in fact, as mentioned above, the children had great responsibility in the household to provide for the family. Their faith in God and in each other resulted in a great gift of interdependence shared throughout the community.

The Gift of Value

Going back to the true responsibility in parenting, we must accept that we are raising adults. They, too, will be facing their own challenges in adulthood and parenthood. The sooner that we can encourage our children to step out and learn their value both personally and societally, the sooner we will watch their confidence and character grow. Then they will be ready to face their own challenges.

As mentioned above, the children in Cercady were trusted with one of the most important chores of the day, gathering water. **Children have great value in the eyes of God**. The psalmist says, "You created my inmost being; you knit me together in my mother's womb" (Psalm 139:13). In Chapter four, we learned that we have a "hands-on God," a God who took great care in the creation of this world. The Psalmist goes on to share "Your eyes saw my unformed body; all the days ordained for me were written in your book before one of them came to be" (Psalm 139:16).

> Not only do we have a "hands-on God," but we have a God who sees us

each individually as someone very special. So special, that he invested in each day of our lives even before they began, according to his word. Remember when you learned to sculpt in art class? Remember the time you spent perfecting each intricate detail of your creation? Now consider the time that God takes to lovingly perfect each intricate detail of your child.

Stop for a moment and soak that in: **God considers us valuable in his kingdom.** When we accept him, we step into his plan, recognizing that we are "children of God." We learned how God loves us so very much to the point of loving through us. The value that he sees in us and in our children is priceless. What would it look like to teach them this—to remind them every day how much God loves them and how they are of great value in his kingdom? What would it look like to remind ourselves of the same truth?

Teaching our children their value inherently encourages a desire to contribute to something greater than themselves. It is in all of us to want to succeed and make a difference in the world in which we live. Recognizing our value in the eyes of our Father encourages much more than a successful life but an opportunity for a significant life.

Can we have a moment of truth here? We all want to be accepted and affirmed. If our children do not learn to find their value in their Heavenly Father, where will they seek acceptance? Too often we build our significance around people and things. We find ourselves sucked into disappointment and discouragement when we don't measure up to others' expectations or even our own. Be reminded, however, that our Father ordained all of our days. My friend, his love for your children is constant, and his acceptance never falters. By teaching them their significance in his eyes, you are giving them a beautiful gift that never expires, breaks, or disappoints.

The Gift of Diligence

Do we allow our children to contribute to the important provisions of the family, or do we tend to provide everything for them? "Lazy hands make for poverty, but diligent hands bring wealth" (Proverbs 10:4). Kevin Queen, one of our campus pastors, shared with us that "God pours out his favor on those who work diligently. Diligence equals excellence, which brings glory to God and an audience of Kings."[14]

As your children learn to contribute to the family, you will find this to be an opportunity to teach the importance of diligence and excellence. This serves not only as a reinforcement of their familial responsibility but even more so encourages them into their active role as valuable and important members. **They realize they have something to offer.** This gift will continually serve them well in their adult life.

The Gift of Serving

One of the greatest gifts we can give is that of serving another. In the book Broken to Broken, Jim Ellison shares with us his story of life and heart change through the beautiful people served by Restoration ATL

---

[14] "Words of Wisdom"—Kevin Queen 5/26/13

(RATL). This is a wonderful ministry serving the homeless women and children of the inner city of Atlanta, Georgia. I had the opportunity to see this ministry in action on a trip with our youth group. There are varying degrees of age and experience in the eyes and hands of each person who walks through their doors, and each one has a story. Some of them are very hard to hear, but all of them are entangled with a grace that we all need and have access to. In Jim's book, he shares something that makes RATL unique. RATL wanted to "seek to help the marginalized in the city experience restoration. The other side of that coin was that restoration would also take place in the lives of those who would come into the city to serve." He goes on to share, "I was aware of my own need for spiritual restoration."[15]

There is something in this that I want you to see. This ministry was choosing to follow the Father's plan of creating a circle of love among both the residents they were serving and those who came to serve. Their motto

---

[15] *Broken to Broken*—Jim Ellison

is to "Be with." Jesus modeled "be with" for us. Those who live in a little town in Cercady, Haiti modeled "be with" for us. And we too need to model "be with" for those whom God has placed in our lives. **Serving is truly the gift that "keeps on giving."**

By limiting the giving of things, teaching our children to have faith, helping them to recognize their value in the Father's eyes, and encouraging them to strive for excellence through diligence and serving others, we find ourselves blessed to watch them grow in both character and integrity. These are gifts not only eternal in nature but pay off in the wealth of a life well lived. Are you unsure if you are giving too much? Would you like to know how to bless your children with eternal gifts? The Book of Proverbs in the Bible is a great place to seek God's wisdom regarding this and other tips on parenting.

Personal Confession

Do you give "things" too much?
Ask God to reveal areas where you may need to give less and mentor/pour into more.

Do you know how special you are to the Father? Do your children know their value? Read Psalm 139:13–18, and soak in his Truth. He loves you so very much and wants you and your child to know that he considers you both valuable to him.

Commit to reading the Book of Proverbs, one chapter per day. Reread every month for one year.

Develop a way to enlist your children to help provide for and give to the family.

Feel free to journal your thoughts here._____

_____

_____

_____   _____

Confessions: A Mom's Journey from Hovering to Hope

CONFESSION #6
I NEED A PAUL AND TIMOTHY IN MY LIFE.

> Chapter 6
> Get Wisdom

A year prior to that expectant November night, God gave me a gift. I heard testimonies of others who were blessed by the prayers and guidance of others through mentorship. I, of course, wanted this for myself but had no idea how to get it.

Then one day, God provided. Her name was Sandy. She was a beautiful kingdom warrior who curiously took me under her wing and taught me to fly.

Have you ever considered your need for a mentor? Prior to this season of my life, I thought I was invincible and ready to take on the world. **I didn't need advice, or did I?**

What is a "mentor"? Dictionary.com describes a mentor as a wise and trusted counselor or teacher.[16]

In The Prideful Soul's Guide to Humility, Michael Fontenot and Thomas Jones tell us:

> "Don't just welcome advice and counsel about parenting; seek it. Go after it like a starving man goes after food. There are still far too many parents who are too prideful to submit to this message. They seem to think that they will do what they think and things will turn out just fine. For a while, it may seem to work out, but then their children hit the preteen and teen years, and it is a whole different story. Had they been getting advice all along, they could have had a

---

[16] www.dictionary.reference.com/browse/mentor

> different result. God would have blessed their humility."

Yes, I fell into this trap and have since recognized the importance of mentorship. Sandy modeled for me the truth that I needed a Paul and Timothy in my life, a Paul I could go to for advice (my parents and close, trusted friends like Sandy), and Timothy that I could mentor (my children and those I lead). Sandy modeled being still before the Lord while lifting intercessory declarations of prayer that completely changed the way I saw the season we were walking through. Her discipleship taught me how faith in the Father *and* his promises would stabilize in the whirlwind of trial.

In Chapter two, we discussed the challenge of making decisions. We learned, in chapter three, how parenting instruction is caught more than taught through our own parents, aka "teachers on the job." We begin to recognize a distinct need to have others in our lives and this is by design. God created us for relationship while placing opportunities in our midst for mentorship. But we must be okay to say, **I need help.** Intentionality is necessary to seek God and those he has placed in our path who may be a few steps ahead. If you find yourself in a place such as this, may I encourage you to prayerfully reach out and ask him to show you the people he has placed in your life who can provide wisdom and guidance? The placement of others in our path is not by accident or mistake. God has a plan.

In Chapter four, we learned how Jesus taught us the meaning of love. When he came to earth, he did so much more than die for our sins. Why did he spend thirty-three years of life in relationship with his creation? Perhaps to teach and model for us true, unconditional love. He showed us that to truly love, you must have relationship. Jesus' investment into those placed in his path set an example for the church, which resulted in the fellowship and "building up" aka "mentorship" that we have access to today.

Consider this:

> Jesus could have come down and said,
> "I Am Almighty God, El Shaddai,

Maker of heaven and earth. Bow down and worship me." He could have, but he didn't. Instead, he chose twelve people to walk with Him, building relationships and teaching them how to live the full life he intended. That was showing relational love at its finest. Over 2,000 years later, we still see the result of his great love for us through the relationships that he has blessed. And even more importantly, we recognize that he is here to mentor and invest in our own lives through a relationship with him, just as he did for the twelve. Our Savior is so good!

When my youngest son was twenty-two and preparing to enter his final year at Georgia Tech, I was once again reminded of this need in my life. He had proven himself to be a responsible young man. So, if this was true, why were my hackles cropping up? Here I was, writing to moms and dads everywhere about finding freedom from hovering, as I found myself succumbing to fear. One thing I found to be true, my Father comforted and reminded me that he was there for me in these moments and his grace was always mine. But I'm getting ahead of myself.

So, in that year my son was working through his first field internship, and there was a situation that cropped up where I felt the need to get involved. In that moment, I remember feeling so strongly about it. I could hear myself saying, "If I don't take **control** of this situation, it will end badly." Wow, there is that ugly word again. Why, in moments of uncertainty do I have these thoughts? Is it pride? Is it fear? Is God trying to work something in and through me?

As I struggled through this moment, I discussed it with a very dear friend of mine, and she stopped me in my tracks with this question, "Why are you not allowing him to handle this?" My first answer was, "He doesn't know what to do." She left me to my thoughts for a moment and came back with this, "Eve, you must allow him to ask his own questions. If you continue to seek and find his answers, he will never know what questions to ask. Are you always going to be with him when he needs to find his own answers?" Ouch—there was wisdom in this question.

God is so very good. **Friend, there are people in your own life who can breathe truth into you**. Allow them to give you this beautiful gift. You don't have to act on every bit that they give you but listen. Pray about it. Ask God to reveal what he wants you to act on and what he wants you to merely consider.

Your Child Needs a Mentor(s.)

After Jesus ascended into heaven, we read in the Book of Acts the story of a budding friendship. Paul was one of the apostles appointed by Jesus. Timothy was a disciple whom Paul found on his second journey. More than once, scripture tells us that Paul calls Timothy his "son in the faith." We watch as Timothy goes with Paul on his second missionary journey; then we see how he is entrusted with ministering to the Church of Ephesus. First and Second Timothy reveals Paul mentoring Timothy in his ministry from afar. The relationship between Paul and Timothy is a wonderful example of God using Paul to pour into Timothy and, likewise, using Timothy to give back.

As you read about this beautiful friendship, you will notice that Paul did not hover. Paul invested in Timothy and sent him out to fulfill his purpose. I am certain that when Timothy needed help making decisions, he would go to Paul who would give him advice. Then Timothy would have to prayerfully move forward and act.

As parents, we have an amazing opportunity to build a relationship with those God has placed in our lives. **God has a plan and uses us to build one another up.** He pours into each of us through those he places in our lives to mentor us, and then we pour into others. And the beautiful circle of love continues.

In Chapter four, we discussed the importance of spending quality time with our children. This is never more critical than in mentorship. As a mentor, we can teach our children the tools they need to be responsible adults, and perhaps more importantly, help them to see their value. This creates a trusting relationship that will last a lifetime. Your child will know they have someone they can come to when life gets hard.

As Jesus traveled, he touched so many people. We learn that he loved each person he poured into. We see that a great deal of time was spent investing in his twelve disciples. How did he pour into them? How can we translate this to mentorship today? To pour means, "to emit or propel, especially continuously."[17] Jesus continuously worked in the lives of his disciples, teaching them how to live the precepts that God gave previously through the Old Testament scriptures. Through his teaching, his love poured out continually. But you will notice that his mentoring of the disciples in person lasted only three years.

In today's society, what does teaching, or mentoring, involve? Not all of us are trained to be teachers-mentors, or are we? In Chapter three, we learned that we are learning from those who came before us while also learning on the job. Some of us can even be misled in the way we should go, passed down by generations of "this is the way my mom/dad did it." So, what if they or we get it wrong? Where do we go from there? Going back to basics is usually a good start.

What does God say about how we should mentor our children?

- Teach your child who God is: God is our Creator (Genesis 1:26; John 1:3; Colossians 1:16). God is our Father (Isaiah 64:8). God is our Savior (Titus 2:13). God is our King (Hebrews 1:2–3). God is love (1 John 4:8).
- Teach your child their worth in the Father's eyes. God says we are fearfully and wonderfully made in his image (Genesis 1:27; Psalm 139:13–16). We are his workmanship created in Christ Jesus for good works (Ephesians 2:10).

---

[17] www.dictionary.reference.com/browse/pour

- Teach your child to trust in the Lord with all their heart (Proverbs 3:5).
- Teach your child to guard their heart (Proverbs 4:23).
- Teach your child to be strong and courageous, not afraid (Joshua 1:9).
- Teach your child they can do all things through Christ who strengthens them (Philippians 4:13).
- Teach your child to get wisdom (Proverbs 4:7–8). Teach your child that it is okay to ask questions. As a wise man once told me, "The only stupid question is the one you didn't ask."
- Teach your child to hope and to dream (Proverbs 13:12).
- Teach your child that God has a purpose and a plan for them (Jeremiah 29:11).
- Teach your child to seek God first with all their heart (Matthew 6:33; Jeremiah 29:13).

- Teach your child that God is our refuge, an ever-present help in times of trouble (Psalm 46:1).
- Teach your child that God will never leave them (Psalm 37:23–24).
- Teach your child to lift their prayers to him when worried and anxious (Philippians 4:6–7).
- Teach your child the two greatest commandments given by Jesus:
  - "Love the Lord your God with all of your heart, soul, and mind," and
  - The second is like it, "Love your neighbor as yourself" (Matthew 22:37-39).

Solomon, the wisest man who lived, shares with us:

> Listen, my son, accept what I say, and the years of your life will be many. I instruct you in the way of wisdom and lead you along straight paths. When you walk, your steps will not be hampered; when you run, you will not stumble.

> Hold on to instruction; do not let it go;
> guard it well, for it is your life"
> (Proverbs 4:10–13).

Notice here that Solomon is instructing, but the responsibility is on the student to fly. In "7 Principles on Developing Leaders," Dan Reiland explains this perfectly: "In mentoring, we are to help those we mentor become their best self, not someone else."[18] Notice the emphasis on "their best self." How many times, as parents, do we pour our ideas, our prejudices, our worries, and our fears into our children? Do we really want them to be just like us? God created each of us as unique individuals with a purpose and a plan for our individual lives.

Do not discount the power of teaching your children their worth. Just as important as teaching them their value in the Father's eyes, it is so important to help your child to recognize they are only limited within the confines of their own mind. Our job is to encourage

---

[18] "7 Principles on Developing Leaders" Blog 7/1/15 DanReiland.com

them to step out of this self-defined box and into the purpose our Father has for them with a promise, "I will instruct you and teach you in the way you should go. I will counsel you with my loving eye on you (Psalm 32:8)."

Through this amazing gift, we find that his love and wisdom pour out continuously. We can be free to transition from hovering to a state of forward flight. We can witness a beautiful transition in the relationships with our children while God reveals their own personal growth. How exciting is this? When you see a butterfly morph from a caterpillar, you have the amazing opportunity to watch creation at work. The same holds true with your children.

I have shared with you only thirteen of God's instructions, but His Word, our "instruction manual," and truly his love letter written to us, is full of instructions on how to raise our children so they can grow into the "life to the full" that he promises (John 10:10b). Our Father, our Flight Instructor and Mentor, is truly the perfect Parent.

Personal Confession

Do you need a Paul? Do you want to learn to mentor your Timothy? Do you allow God's Word to help you in decision-making?

Ask God to lead you to those in your life who can mentor you. Pray that he will teach you how to mentor your own children.

Seek his wisdom every day in his Word.

Make a list of items from God's Word to teach your children.

Commit to encouraging your children to learn one per week.

Feel free to journal your thoughts here.

_____   _____

_____

_____

_____

Confessions: A Mom's Journey from Hovering to Hope

CONFESSION #7
I FIND IT HARD TO LET GO.

> Chapter 7
> Learning to Let Go

Yes, letting go is hard for me. I have spent too many anxious moments and sleepless nights in worry over what would happen if I let go. Much like a search-and-rescue effort, I would find myself searching for the unexpected spins in life while preparing to rescue the outcome. Whether encouraging them to take their first step, removing the training wheels, watching them drive off in their first car, or moving them into college, letting go always seemed irresponsible to me. My thought process: God gave me a task as a parent, and I would be remiss in neglecting my duty if I let them make their own choices and mistakes. Ergo, "Mommy fix-it-mode." OUCH again!

This is a good segue into the hope-full November night in which everything changed. A night when every lesson that came before would be brought home. As we walked the prayer trail, I could feel the weight of the calling on my husband and me. Our son was in crisis, and it was time to let him go while trusting God to direct his path.

That night we were interceding for our son. You see, he had been walking a very dark path that led to drug abuse and isolation from family. We felt helpless. There was only One who could help him, and so on that hope-filled night, we joined others at the throne of God and laid our son at the feet of Jesus.

Three short months later, we had the answer to our prayer. It was a Monday when I received the call, "Mom, I'm in jail."

"What happened, Son?"

"I can't talk about it over the phone, Mom."

I was broken. No longer was I looking at chips flying around through the whirlwind of our circumstances. I was dodging shards of glass flying from all directions. "God, how could you let this happen?" I prayed. God, in His loving way, said, "Eve, I've got him. You can trust me."

Guess what I did? I let go. Well, somewhat . . .

As parents, we have a great responsibility for the rearing of our children. **While it is true that we must teach them to walk, we must allow them to do the walking.**

Jesus modeled letting go for us. You will notice that he never stayed in one place for long. He was consistently traveling from town to town, teaching, and loving others, then moving to the next place. Pouring into the vessel allows the vessel to pour into others. Jesus chose to move from place to place, sharing his Word with those he met, while encouraging them to further pour into others. At the perfect moment, Jesus would release his disciples into apostleship to continue the task he had started.

Imagine if he had hovered over those that he mentored? Would he have had the chance to touch so many people? Would those he influenced have had the courage to pour into others? Thankfully, he didn't hover but instead taught them how to faithfully step out into their own purpose.

Just as Jesus pushed forward in the purpose given him, we must also propel forward and release our precious children into the hands of the God who knew them first. In Chapter two, we discussed free will, choice, and how often we choose our will over God's. God taught us a valuable lesson about letting our children make their own decisions in the story of Adam and Eve Through my own journey, I learned that letting a child go takes prayer, wisdom, discernment, and, of course, trust that their Creator will help them when the going gets tough.

Consider this for a moment, with the understanding that we are raising adults, how important is it to allow our children to make their own decisions, choices, and even mistakes? I'll share some revolutionary advice from my aunt with you: "Give them permission to fail." Yes, I said fail. Remember those challenges that seemingly served to break us in the moment? As difficult as it is to admit, these challenges serve to motivate us to become strong, humble, and wise. You might think of them as muscle-builders. Just as a squat has to tear down the muscle to build it, so our challenges serve to strengthen the muscles of faith, confidence, and grit. By hovering over our children, we may be guarding them from harm, pain, and loss—with good intentions of course. However, we could also be innocently participating in stunting their character growth.

Character growth is personal and intentional. It must be fostered in a healthy environment of love and mentoring. When you allow the child to see him or herself as God sees them, and teach them to seek his purpose and plan in all they do, you free them up to trust God to build their confidence and courage to face the difficulties of this world. Dan Reiland shares in his book, Amplified Leadership, "Life will present plenty of hardships, and learning how to deal with those challenges will help my children develop wisdom and character. This inner strength will enable them to handle the even tougher situations that will come their way."[19] However, this is not without challenges.

Consider a bodybuilder. It takes great effort, patience, and time to build a healthy body. Wouldn't we all like to have the "magic pill" to find ourselves in tip-top shape? However, the true gift in this effort is the perseverance, knowledge, and experience gained along the way. When you persevere through the challenges and the pain, you see long-lasting success in the building of muscles. The result is a strong body, yes, but even more so the character and the strength built in the process. We must understand, just as in building a strong body, that building character takes a lifetime. Our lives and the

---

[19] *Amplified Leadership*—Dan Reiland

lives of our children are a work in progress from birth to death.

One of the gifts of parenting is that we can watch God build character in our children while building character within us. Yes, it can be painful at times to watch them experience pain or even spiral into failure. But just as in the work of the bodybuilder, the result of every character-building block is a strong character that is dependent on God.

We discussed how God demonstrated this first with Adam and Eve. Why did he do that? Why was it necessary to allow free will to take place? Well, consider this, if God had created a world full of robots programmed to perform his every whim, would we ever choose him? In God's perfect semblance of love, he gave us free will and allowed us the freedom of choice so that we would recognize his love was greater than anything we could ever find on our own.

The story of the Prodigal Son demonstrates a father's love expressed within letting his son go. In this story, a young man comes of age and decides to ask for his inheritance so he can leave home. He is the second son in the home and chooses to move far away and squander his inheritance. When he is left with nothing, his only choice is to eat with the pigs, yes, the pigs. He has a moment that I believe we all have in our lives—a moment when he realizes that a lifetime of dependence on a loving father is greater than a lifetime of independence alone. He decides to return home and ask his father to make him a servant in the household. As he is returning home, the father is waiting and watching for his lost son. He sees his son from far away and, without a second thought, begins running to meet him. You see, the son thought that all was lost, but the father accepted him back into the family as his son, even throwing a party in his honor (Luke 15:11–32). Our Father instructs us how to live our lives; then he gives us free will to make our own choices, good or bad. And if we turn away from him, he is waiting with open arms for us to return. Friend, he gives us the love and the strength to do the same for our own children.

I had to recognize this truth on that cold November night. Yes, I spent twenty-one years as a parent, making a lot of mistakes, but my son's Creator knew him way before I did. He entrusted us with his care while preparing us for the moment when we would pray for a miracle. Now what you must know is that God's ways are not our ways, and I would soon learn that he does not answer our prayers as we would desire. When I watched my prodigal as he was led off to prison, I felt as if that baby that I was so afraid to carry was being ripped out of my arms. Yes, all the worries in that first nine months of pregnancy came roaring back to me.

However, the Creator of the universe, the One who is Love; the same One who accepts us when we turn away from him, held me in his arms. He proceeded to not only heal my heart from the pain of temporarily losing a loved one but assured me of these truths: **God is bigger than any storm.** He is greater than any challenge we face. When we let go and let him lead, he lifts us above our challenges while reminding us that his grace is sufficient to bring us through the storm.

There is a story of Jesus and his disciples in Mark 4:35–41 where, after a long day, they were crossing the Sea of Galilee. Jesus was asleep on a pillow in the stern of the boat. As they were crossing, a storm rolled in. Mark describes it as "a furious squall." Imagine the scene: Jesus is asleep, and waves are crashing over the boat, so much so that the boat was taking on water. The disciples, we notice, are quite concerned; they wake Jesus with an anxious tone, "Teacher, don't you care if we drown?"

> Have you ever had a moment when a challenge in life swirls like a tornado around you, suffocating and spiraling you down into a tailspin? It is easy to feel like there is no way out as you yell, "Mayday! Mayday!" Anxiety and worry can seem like familiar friends in these moments.

As the disciples are worried about their immediate future, Jesus stands up, rebukes the wind, and says to the waves, "Quiet! Be still!" Then Mark tells us that the wind died down, and it was completely calm. Take note here: Mark didn't say that the storm decreased. He said, "It was completely calm."

Jesus Is Greater Than the Storm.

Just as Jesus calmed the storm completely and immediately for the disciples, he can do the same for you. When the challenges hit, when the anxiety rises, at this moment, be still and remember:

Jesus Is Greater Than Your Storm.

This comforting truth is for each of us. For me to believe that I was solely responsible for stunting the growth in my son's character was to think that I was greater than the Creator of the universe. Did I remind my son to do his homework? Yes. Did I naively hover, thinking that I was responsible for his character growth? I can answer this with a resounding yes. However, was I responsible for his choices? No. What I learned through this challenge, (and continue to learn even to this day), is that my son was and is responsible for his choices. More importantly, I had to recognize that God's plan was greater than mine, and I had to relinquish control over him. We love our children, we use the tools we are given to teach them, but ultimately, they must make their own way. While I may have hovered for many years, once my son became an adult, I was not responsible for any of his choices. And neither are you responsible for your children's choices.

Let me say that again, neither are you.

This is the crux of parenthood. Remember when I said that we aren't raising children, but we are raising adults? For our children to grow to love, to have wisdom, and to make good choices, they too must face their own challenges in life and make their own good and bad choices—and accept their consequence(s).

My friend, can we have a personal moment? You can do all the right things and still experience challenges in parenting. We live in a world where the enemy would like nothing more than to steal our joy and take us out.

The enemy does not want us to raise children dependent on the Father because he knows that this is where our peace and our strength come from. He would much rather find us weak, defenseless, and beaten down. Your Father loves you and your children so very much and has promised that he will protect you from trouble (Psalm 32:7). This is not a promise that trouble will never find you or your child but only that he will guide you through it. In these moments when the storm is ever looming, stop and pray. Pray for his peace, pray for his wisdom, and pray for his comfort. And know that in this moment I am praying for you, praying that you will give your heart to him and allow him to comfort you and give you strength and wisdom through all challenges that you face.

There is great beauty in this. Your children will not only have a chance to learn who they are in the eyes of the Father, but they will also learn how God wants them to live their life. Through every choice, right or wrong, bad, or good, God will build their character bit by bit, teaching them to navigate with him as their Air Traffic Controller on their own forward flight. And he will love them through it all. They, too, will learn that dependence on God is greater than independence alone, just as the prodigal son learned.

For those of us, who have many years of parenthood behind us, know that this truth is for us as well. It may be time to release our children into adulthood. There may be fear in our hearts that we may not have done everything "right." But every morning, God gives us a new do-over. "Because of the Lord's great love we are not consumed, for his compassions never fail. They are new every morning; great is your faithfulness" (Lamentations 3:22–23; emphasis added). Today is a brand-new day friend. Give your child to the Father and ask him to show you how to trust him and move forward in his grace. His grace is sufficient, and his power is made perfect in our weakness (2 Corinthians 12:9)!

There is a beautiful online video of a giraffe giving birth in a Miami zoo. Immediately after the baby is born, it lays on the ground, completely immobile. The momma giraffe takes a moment to lick her new baby awake. We then watch as the baby giraffe courageously works up the strength to stand. Within minutes, the sweet babe is wobbling on all fours. We then watch as the momma pushes her baby forward. Our God does the same for us. He loves us and propels us forward into the life he has for us with a promise, "I am with you always, to the very end of the age" (Matthew 28:20b), all the while lovingly teaching us to do the same for our own children.

In the season that I had to push my son forward, I watched God do miraculous things as he drew him near. Not only did my son come home, but he came home clean and with purpose! God not only restored the years the locusts had eaten but faithfully showed us how he reveals before he heals. I can rest in the truth that God does meet all our needs according to the riches of his glory in Christ Jesus (Philippians 4:19). But Friend, I had to let go to learn this truth.

Can I encourage you with this? The same God who gave us his holy Word to guide and direct us in life, the same God who called the sun and the stars into being, the same God who held me in his righteous right hand in my fear and worries over my son, the same God who brought this sweet young giraffe into the world is the same God who will hold your child as well when you give them back to him.

Personal Confession

Where do you need to let go?

Ask God to give you the courage to let go and trust that his plan is greater than your own.

Pray that he will protect your children, guide, and direct them, and give you the wisdom to teach them how to walk while giving you the patience to let them walk.

Feel free to journal your thoughts here.

_____

_____

_____

_____

_____

_____

_____

Confessions: A Mom's Journey from Hovering to Hope

CONFESSION #8
IT'S HARD TO LEAVE MY NEATLY PLANNED PATH.

> Chapter 8
> Learning to Enjoy the Adventure

Have you ever gone on an adventure? I'll admit, as a mom it's hard to consider the thought of going on an unplanned adventure. When we went on our first real family vacation, I was so excited! I had everything planned for the week, to the minute. When my husband offered to trade spontaneity for my neatly planned schedule, I was quite frustrated. What if we missed our reservations? What if we didn't get to experience all the fun things I had carefully planned? What if nobody had fun? What if? What if? I will share that I spent hours frustrated over the what-ifs. And in so doing, I missed quite a bit of fun myself.

My boys didn't know about all the great excursions I had planned; they only knew that they were on a great adventure. In their adventure, they were able to walk floors that defied the eye and cover each other in man-sized bubbles. They had great fun, but it was not part of my carefully planned schedule. How many times and for what reason have I done this; I wonder? As I get older, I find that through careful planning, the day goes as expected and I "suffer" few surprises. But I also miss the beautiful surprises awaiting me.

As children, we love surprises. Surprises bring us joy and allow us to write memories, which we could never plan. These are the exciting moments of great journal entries and great life stories. What happens when we become parents? Surprises interrupt the carefully controlled plan that we have created. Ouch! There's that word again—control. So, what does the Bible say about our plans? "In their hearts, humans plan their course, but the Lord establishes their steps" (Proverbs 16:9).

As we recognized in Chapter two, our Father gave Adam and Eve the choice to make their own decisions. He also gives us free will to do the same. In planning our course, we learn something significant, following him allows us to live in his promise. **His promise is to give us hope and a future, fill us with joy, and give us life to the full.** When we follow him, read his Word, and prayerfully seek his guidance he establishes our steps. And when we give our children back to him, he can also establish their steps.

By allowing myself to be frustrated over my perfect plans being foiled, I was showing that I was frustrated about losing control, and the only one who lost in this was me. I think what God is sharing in this perfect verse is to recognize once again that he places us in charge, but he is in control. We need only to trust him and be free to follow his detours. Don't be afraid of surprises. Allow him to interrupt our plans and guide us on a beautiful journey.

When we learn to loosen our grip and leave our own beaten path, accepting his perfect plan, we give God the opportunity to be our Navigator as he reveals the beauty of his creation. Remember the surprises which were so much fun as a child? Our Father wants to surprise us every day, even now. This is evident in the palette he paints for us in every sunrise and sunset and in the beauty of every blooming flower. Breathe in the life he has for you. Just as he breathed life into the first man in Genesis, he wants to breathe life into you every day. Be still and allow him to pour this into you. Our Heavenly Father has created an everyday blessing just for you.

The life to the full that Jesus promised isn't just for our children, but for us as well. God doesn't want us to live a life of stress, worry, and anxiety. He wants us to wake up every day and enjoy the beauty he has created just for us. My friend, may I encourage you, beginning tomorrow, to resist the snooze button and allow our Father to reveal the beauty of his creation to you. Let him be your tour guide on a grand adventure.

Remember that his detour is your blessing. Enjoy each surprise that he longs to share with you and teach your children to seek their own blessings as well.

Personal Confession

Where do you need to release control?

Ask God to reveal this to you and to help you to release control to him.

Pray that he will open your eyes to the beauty of following his detour and enjoying his surprises.

Feel free to journal your thoughts here.

_____

_____

_____

_____

_____

_____

_____

_____

_____

Confessions: A Mom's Journey from Hovering to Hope

CONFESSION #9
I AM A WORK IN PROGRESS AND AM
PRAYERFULLY TRUSTING GOD TO HELP ME
TO BE THE PARENT HE ENTRUSTED WITH MY
CHILDREN.

Chapter 9
Freedom!

Parenthood doesn't have to be just a responsibility, but it is, in fact, a gift given to us by our perfect Father. We have a choice to hold tight and risk a crash-and-burn, or we can trust our Father to provide, instruct, protect, and comfort us as we learn to give—and dedicate—our children back to him through these most challenging years. His Power gives us freedom to live, and his peace is ours.

In summary, how can we live a life free from hovering?

First, recognize that God teaches us to appreciate that children are a heritage from the Lord. Our offspring are a reward from our Father (Psalm 127:3).

Parenting is a gift that allows us to see his love in action, both in and through us. As our perfect example, we know we can look to him for help in the small and large decisions in our lives.

Through God, we can control our thoughts and guard our hearts. Give the Father the first of our day and our thoughts and allow him to bless the rest. Allow those who came before: our parents, grandparents, and great-grandparents to invest in us and our children. Ask questions. We can learn so much from those who have come before us. Remember that they probably have gone through many things that we have yet to go through.

Make communication key in your family. Include your spouse in all decisions and communicate them clearly to your children. Recognize and accept that being a parent is hard work. Understand that with any challenge comes strength and growth of character. Nothing good comes easily, and parenting is no exception, but you can trust God to provide in for all things.

Teach your children that we all have a choice and that there is a consequence for every choice whether good or bad. Give yourself and your children the permission to fail. Accept that we will fail at some point in our lives and know that we have a Father who will help us when we fall. We can feel secure that we will rise from the failure, propel forward, and learn from the challenge. The only true failure is when we fail to try again. Rely on God's Word to help with the easy and the difficult decisions. The Bible is chock-full of wisdom and guidance for the raising of our children. This is and always will be our greatest instruction manual. Find a handful of verses that you can memorize to help you through the tough challenges you face. Mine is Philippians 4:13, what is yours?

Do not worry or be anxious about parenting. An anxious heart breeds an anxious mind, which brings chaos and unhappiness, taking away the peace provided by our Father who is always here for us in our time of need. Remember, he entrusted you with your children by placing you in charge; trust that he knows what he is doing and will give you the strength you need in parenting. This will go a long way toward healing an anxious heart. He promises when we learn to, "not be anxious about anything, but in every situation, by prayer and petition, with thanksgiving, present your requests to God. The peace of God which transcends all understanding will guard our hearts and minds in Christ Jesus" (Philippians 4:6–7). Friend, this was true yesterday, is true today, and will continue to be true tomorrow.

Remember that God is Love and the Source of our love. We have a Creator, a Father who is hands-on and loves us unconditionally. He loved us first and loves through us. His unconditional love gives us the strength to persevere.

Seek a Godly mentor, someone whom you trust and who will not only listen but will encourage you to be your "best self." Commit to do the same for your own children.

Bless your children with the eternal gifts of faith, value, diligence and serving. Faith that God will provide in all things, value as seen through the Father's eyes, diligence in all they do and learning to give ourselves away. As we watched Jesus give himself away in the New Testament, we too can teach our children a beautiful lesson by giving our time to them and to others. The sharing of love and compassion with those God has placed in our lives creates memories that our children will carry with them for the rest of their lives, not to mention teaching them to pass it forward.

Trust in your Father to help you. Allowing God to take the reign and be in control brings great freedom. You can trust him. The same God who created the universe, who knitted your child in their mother's womb, and who knew them before they were created can be trusted with their life. But this requires giving them back to him, using the tools he has given to encourage them to see who they are in his eyes, and teaching them how to follow his Word. These gifts will help them to make choices allowing for the purpose and plan he designed just for them. And don't forget to pray, pray, pray! The power of prayer is huge, and God has given your child a beautiful gift in you. You can serve as your child's greatest prayer warrior!

Finally, relax and enjoy parenthood. Seek his daily blessings. Remember that life is a journey, an adventure. His plan is greater than any plan we can create on our own. God gave us this great gift as an opportunity to see his love in action firsthand. In watching our children grow, we get to see a small glimpse into the heart of our Creator for his creation, not to mention watching them learn to navigate the beauty of their own adventure.

Friends, we don't have to get lost in the fear, worry, and insecurities that serve to distract us from the life to the full we have been promised. His strength is ours; his love is ours, and his joy is ours; we only have to reach out and receive these gifts he has given us. I hope that your journey will be as beautiful as my own and that you will experience the life to the full that Jesus promised.

For me, well, let's just say that the helicopter has landed for now. Dependent on my Father and his will for our family, I know that I can dwell in his shelter and rest in his shadow.

I think I'll leave the helipad and find a beach.

Personal Confession

What is the one thing God is calling you to?

Is it to trust him?

Is it to spend more time in devotion and prayer seeking his wisdom for you and your children?

Is it to seek a Mentor?

Is it to release your anxious heart to Him?

Is it to rest and enjoy the life to the full he has promised?

Ask him to give you the wisdom to be the parent he has called you to be and the strength to step out in faith, accepting this beautiful gift he has given you.

Feel free to journal your thoughts here.

_____

_____

Confessions: A Mom's Journey from Hovering to Hope

CONFESSION #10—NOW THE REST OF THE STORY.

Chapter 10
Redemption

Eight years ago, I set out to write my first book, Confession of a Helicopter Mom. It is said that an author always has that one book that needs a rewrite. This is my *first* rewrite. (Emphasis on first.)

I received a review that weighed heavily on me. The reviewer shared that I had only scratched the surface and that I needed to expound on my personal stories. At the time, I wasn't sure I could go there, but today I am happy to be able to tell the rest of the story. Oh, and by the way, I love constructive feedback. So thank you to the reviewer!

In chapter five, I shared a story about my first mission trip to Cercady, Haiti. I shared how they had no running water. Well, I am happy to report that God has answered this prayer. Here is an excerpt from 410Bridge written in 2019: "The water project in Cercady community is still very successful. The people from this community still testify about this drinking water system that water mission implemented in this community. They said that years ago, there were so many kids who used to get sick from the water due to being unsafe but because of the water system and access to safe drinking water, many children are not becoming sick."[20] Praise God for answered prayer! They do still need a health care center, please join me in praying that God will fulfill this need as well.

In chapter seven, I touched on my son's stay in prison. The night my husband and I walked the prayer trail in 2011, we were interceding for our son. You see, he was addicted to drugs, and we felt helpless. There was only

---

[20] https://www.410bridge.org/cercady-community-update/

One who could help him, and so we laid him at the Lord's feet.

Three short months later, we had our answer. It was a Monday when I received the call, "Mom, I'm in jail."

"What happened, Son?"

"I can't talk about it over the phone, but know I was helping a friend."

When I watched my son led away in zip ties, I died inside. Nineteen-year-old me screamed, "What did I do wrong, God?" But God, in His loving way said, "Eve, I've got him. You can trust me."

You may wonder what we prayed. Honestly, it was a dangerous prayer, "God, please, please heal my son. Whatever it takes." You see, this is a prayer of surrender. "Whatever it takes" means that you may watch your adult child reach their bottom. But Friend, the beauty of the bottom is that there is only one way to look, UP. Please do not misunderstand, surrender IS NOT the same as giving up. Surrender is giving your child to the One who formed them in their mother's womb. Surrender is choosing not to enable them, but to allow them to experience and ***grow from*** their individual consequences. And surrender is trusting God to lead your child into his way everlasting- his way, not ours.

Over the course of the days, weeks, months, and eight years that followed, we navigated the helicopter's tailwind fully connected to our Stabilizer. Our weekends were spent traveling up to six hours to visit him. We traded the freedom of empty nesting for an eight-year winter season of prayerful waiting. But can I share that the Lord had us in his hand. Visit after visit, we watched other parents, spouses, and children fight their own battles. We were not alone. And in that beautiful season, we witnessed the planting of a seed in our son that God watered and cultivated into his spring reveal.

It has been eleven years since that day of November Hope. And today I am gratefully celebrating my son's graduation from Regeneration. God brought us all through the fire and beautifully rolled out the gift of redemption for my son. He is a responsible young man with a caring heart and a strong work ethic. He is living out his identity in Christ and receiving the grace God has for him. I cried tears of joy when I heard him tell his testimony. You see, the reason I couldn't share the whole story eight years ago, was because it was his story. But he has given me permission to share, so here I am. One day, I pray he will write his own accounting, but for now, you have the accounting of a recovering hovering mom who has surrendered her son to the King and watched her prodigal come home.

I know that every day is a gift that I do not take for granted. I praise my God for my son's healing as I pray for his protection. I recognize the temptations of this world are still strong.

But my God is stronger.

Friend, when I sat down to write this book, I wanted so very much to share in the goodness of God and what he had done for this naïve, unqualified momma. Parenting isn't easy, but God is good, and he entrusted us with our children. He knows what he is doing, even if and when I do not.

Perhaps you've noticed that I renamed this labor of love. The common theme that God blessed this hovering mom with over and over in the last eleven years was "HOPE." This wasn't a coincidence but was a resounding confirmation of his word. The hope of God is real.

I don't know where you are in your parenting journey, but I would like to encourage you with this: God entrusted you with your child/children. He doesn't make mistakes. HE CHOSE YOU and he will never leave you nor forsake you. My friend, he sees you and your children, and he loves you dearly. He hears your prayers. He will provide for all your needs according to the riches of his glory in Christ Jesus. And yes, you too can trust our Abba Father to make all things for your family's good and for his glory.

If you are struggling today, know that I believe in you and am praying for God's hope to surround you and your loved one. Please accept this blessing from our Father.

> MAY THE LORD BLESS YOU AND KEEP YOU.
>
> MAY HE MAKE HIS FACE TO SHINE UPON YOU AND BE GRACIOUS TO YOU.
>
> MAY HE TURN HIS FACE TO YOU AND GIVE YOU HIS PERFECT PEACE.

Personal Confession

God has entrusted you with your children, take this section and write a letter of thanks to Him. Share all the many blessings you have been given in and through your children. And praise Him, for he is good.

I will do the same.

_____

_____

_____

_____

_____

_____

_____

_____

_____

Confessions: A Mom's Journey from Hovering to Hope

FINAL THOUGHTS

When I obediently stepped out to share our story, I had no idea the seeds that God would plant and the harvest to follow.

Scripture is very clear about confession. We aren't called to privately confess to God ONLY, but also to one another. It is healing, both physically and spiritually. Confession releases the grace of God and the power of God into our situation. It also connects us one to another. Just as God taught me the beauty of unity in communication, he is teaching me the beauty of confession.

My family's story is still being written. And each day is a revelation of the faithfulness and love of our Father. I am so very thankful for His investment in our parenting.

Thank you to everyone who has surrounded our family with grace and intercession. Thank you for the encouragement that has spurred us on to complete the race to which we have been called.

We love you all.

About The Author

Eve Harrell is a wife and mother living in Lawrenceville, Georgia. Eve and her high school sweetheart Tony have been married for thirty-two wonderful years. Blessed with two amazing sons, Lee and Lance, God has fulfilled his promises over and over in their family. Eve and Tony serve in the high school ministry at 12Stone® Church in Lawrenceville, Georgia and are thankful for the blessings God continues to share as he pours into others, changes hearts, and brings peace to the next generation.

Eve enjoys writing, songwriting, blogging, and helping others find the great love and freedom that Jesus has for them.

Her works can be found at www.adaughtersjourney.net.

As the rain and the snow come down from heaven, and do not return to it without watering the earth and making it bud and flourish, so that it yields seed for the sower and bread for the eater, so is my Word that goes out from my mouth, It will not return to me empty, but will accomplish what I desire and achieve the purpose for which I sent it. You will go out in joy and be led forth in peace; the mountains and hills will burst into song before you, and all the trees of the field will clap their hands. (Isaiah 55:10–12)

May God establish our steps.

Additional works from Eve M. Harrell

Hello Beautiful:
See Yourself Through the Father's Eyes

Hello Beautiful:
Companion Journal

Running with Zebras:
A Daughter's Journey Through the Fire

Revealed Truth:
A Journey from Fear to Faith

Father,

I pray for every parent reading this book. I pray, Lord, that you will grant them the freedom to fully trust in you. I pray, Father, that we will all know the life to the full that you have planned for each of us. I pray for wisdom and discernment as we learn to love our children as we are called. I lift all our children to you and ask that you guide and direct them. Give them great wisdom to face the challenges and trials in their lives. Allow us the beauty of watching them grow into the persons you designed them to be. Thank you for allowing us to see your love in the eyes of our children.

In Jesus' Name,

Amen.

Made in the USA
Columbia, SC
28 May 2025